Cecilia McDowall

Music of the Stars

for SATB and piano or strings and percussion

vocal score

OXFORD
UNIVERSITY PRESS

OXFORD
UNIVERSITY PRESS

Great Clarendon Street, Oxford OX2 6DP,
United Kingdom

Oxford University Press is a department of the University of Oxford.
It furthers the University's objective of excellence in research, scholarship,
and education by publishing worldwide. Oxford is a registered trade mark of
Oxford University Press in the UK and in certain other countries

First published 2023

Impression: 1

ISBN 978–0–19–356428–2

Music origination by Anna Williams
Text origination by Katie Johnston

Printed in Great Britain on acid-free paper by
Halstan & Co. Ltd, Amersham, Bucks.

Contents

Duration: 13 minutes

Instrumentation

percussion—1 player (vibraphone, glockenspiel, suspended cymbal)
strings

Full scores and instrumental parts are available on hire/rental.

If required, the work may also be accompanied by piano, playing from the vocal score.

Composer's note

Music of the Stars was commissioned by long-time Chamber Singers of Iowa City member, James Petersen, and his spouse, David McCartney, to celebrate the Chamber Singers' fiftieth season.

James and David suggested a commission which could celebrate the power of music in these difficult times. I was most touched to be offered such a rewarding opportunity. Finding just the right text to set is such an interesting process and I felt this one was particularly engaging. In recognition of the racial issues which face us every day, the commissioners and music director, David Puderbaugh, offered texts written by people of colour: James Weldon Johnson and Kenyan-born Brian Odongo. The latter text was discovered by another CSIC singer, Elaine Reding. To continue the theme of music, singing, and the stars, I discovered an absorbing explanation of 'light' and how we perceive it by the American astrophysicist Neil deGrasse Tyson. He is an outstanding science communicator and I found myself drawn to and fascinated by his planetary postings, which have a clarity I had not encountered before.

The atmospheric text of the first movement, 'Music of the Stars', evokes 'dark night clouds', illuminated by ancient, radiant stars as they watch over mortals' adventures below; the 'music of the stars' sings to 'seafarers, wayfarers, and soldiers'. There is a gentle, almost mesmerizing pace to the poem which I hope is reflected in the music. I wove just a small part of a Ukrainian folksong into this movement—*In the garden flowers are growing, Boys will quarrel where I'm going*—as it just seemed impossible to ignore the unfolding horror in Ukraine. I would be mortified if this seemed a posturing gesture but as I was writing I found it hard not to be affected by these shocking events and to feel, at the same time, utterly powerless as a witness.

In the text of the second, up-tempo movement, 'The hardest thing', Tyson explores the concept of how we analyse colour. Certainly, when reading Tyson's explanation of how the universe is studied, one begins to sense what an extraordinarily complex science astrophysics is. Setting prose to music needs a different approach, I feel, and I aimed to bring a more conversational style to the word setting, sometimes repeating the little phrase endings, to give a little more emphasis.

The poem 'The Gift to Sing' will be so familiar to many. I found this a wonderful poem to set; there is something so quietly confident, so intimate and ultimately joyful about it. Each verse ends with a solution to the day's challenges—'I softly sing'; 'And sing, and sing'; 'And I can sing'. These heart-warming words bring an affirmation of what the power of singing can do for us all in times of difficulty. The text speaks to us all in these most exacting times. How glorious it is, at last, to sing again. I do hope this work brings a response to the times in which we now live.

This note may be reproduced as required for programme notes.

Texts

1. Music of the Stars

The dark night clouds are starlit
As though to mock the moon
That arises at each twilight
To take the mantle from the sun
All united in an assignment
To light the dark auditorium below
The radiant stars gloriously move
Age to age whispering its adventures
It's the music of the stars
Singing the past, present and future
Singing a past heard in legends
Singing a present felt by all men
Singing a future obscure to mortals
It's the music of the stars.

The inaudible lyrics of the stars
That need neither lute nor lyre
To arouse the heart with its ancient rhyme
That chime that is older than any note
Like a spell enchants the audience.

Its melody wanes towards daybreak
Like a script come to a timely end
Its rhythm diminishes
Like the beats fleeting from dawn
Its harmony disaccords
Like harpers' strings breaking,
Singing a ballad to seafarers
Singing a hymn to wayfarers
Singing an anthem to soldiers
It's the music of the stars.

Brian Odongo (b. 1994), adap.
© Brian Odongo. Used by permission.

*Ukrainian folksong

**In the garden flowers are growing,
Boys will quarrel where I'm going.*

v

2. The hardest thing

The hardest thing, I think, by far, is how we analyze spectra—light broken up into its component colors. It's so abstract, so removed from the actual object we are studying. See, chemists study chemicals in the lab. See, biologists study life on Earth. But astrophysicists can't grab a piece of a galaxy and put it in a laboratory. We have to study a picture of the thing, and then analyze the light that comes from it. Nearly everything we know about the machinery of our universe comes to us through the analysis of light. It's all just light—and ninety-nine percent of it happens to be invisible to the naked eye.

Neil deGrasse Tyson (b. 1958), adap.

3. The Gift to Sing

Sometimes the mist overhangs my path,
And blackening clouds about me cling;
But, oh, I have a magic way
To turn the gloom to cheerful day—
    I softly sing.

And if the way grows darker still,
Shadowed by Sorrow's somber wing,
With glad defiance in my throat,
I pierce the darkness with a note,
    And sing, and sing.

I brood not over the broken past,
Nor dread whatever time may bring;
No nights are dark, no days are long,
While in my heart there swells a song,
    And I can sing.

James Weldon Johnson (1871–1938)

Commissioned for the Chamber Singers of Iowa City, David Puderbaugh, Music Director,
by James Petersen and David McCartney on the occasion of the choir's 50th anniversary season

Music of the Stars

CECILIA McDOWALL

1. Music of the Stars

Brian Odongo (b. 1994), adap.

The dark night clouds are star-lit As though to mock the

The dark night clouds are star-lit As though to mock the

2

whis-per-ing,

whis-per-ing,

whis-per-ing its ad-ven-tures, its ad-ven-tures, whis-per-ing, whis-per-ing,

whis-per-ing its ad-ven-tures, its ad-ven-tures, whis-per-ing, whis-per-ing, whis-per-ing,

whis-per-ing, It's the mu-sic of the stars, the mu-sic

It's the mu-sic of the stars, the mu-sic

whis-per-ing, It's the mu-sic of the stars, the mu-sic

the mu-sic

*Ukrainian folksong

To a-rouse the heart with its an - cient rhyme___ That chime that is

To a-rouse the heart with its an - cient rhyme___ That chime that is

Boys___ will quar - rel___ where I'm go - ing.___

Boys will quar - rel___ where I'm go - ing.___

old - er___ than a - ny note___

old - er___ than a - ny note___

Like a spell___ en - chants the au-di-ence.

Like a spell___ en - chants the au-di-ence.

Its me-lo-dy wanes to-wards day-break Like a

Its me-lo-dy wanes to-wards day-break Like a

script,___ a script,

script,___ a script,

Like a script, like a script come to a time-ly___ end_____

Like a script, like a script come to a time-ly___ end_____

2. The hardest thing

Neil deGrasse Tyson (b. 1958), adap.

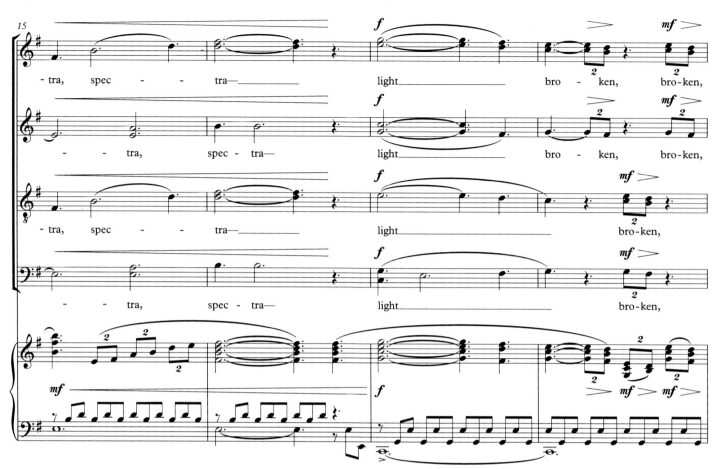

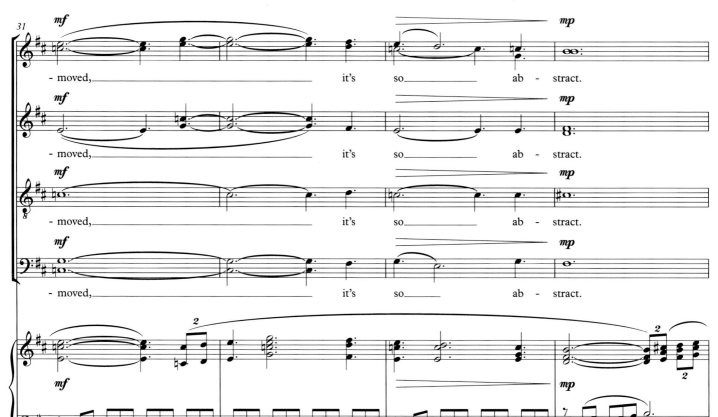

-moved, it's so ab - stract.

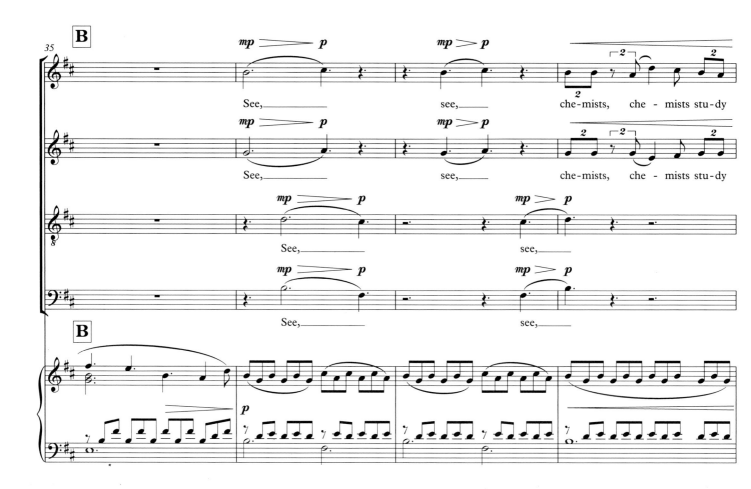

B

See, see, che-mists, che - mists stu-dy

See, see, che-mists, che - mists stu-dy

See, see,

See, see,

che-mi-cals in the lab. See, see,

che-mi-cals in the lab. See, see,

see, lab. See, see,

see, lab. See, see,

bi - o - lo-gists stu - dy, stu - dy life on Earth.

bi - o - lo-gists stu - dy, stu - dy life on Earth.

bi - o - lo-gists stu - dy, stu - dy life on Earth.

bi - o - lo-gists stu - dy, stu - dy life on Earth.

comes to us through the a-na-ly-sis of light, a-na-ly-sis of
comes to us through the a-na-ly-sis of light, a-na-ly-sis of
a - na-ly-sis of light.
a - na-ly-sis of light.

light. It's all just light— and nine-ty-nine per-cent of it hap-pens to
light. It's all just light— and nine-ty-nine per-cent of it hap-pens to
It's all just light— and nine-ty-nine per-cent of it hap-pens to
It's all just light— and nine-ty-nine per-cent of it hap-pens to

3. The Gift to Sing

James Weldon Johnson (1871–1938)

26

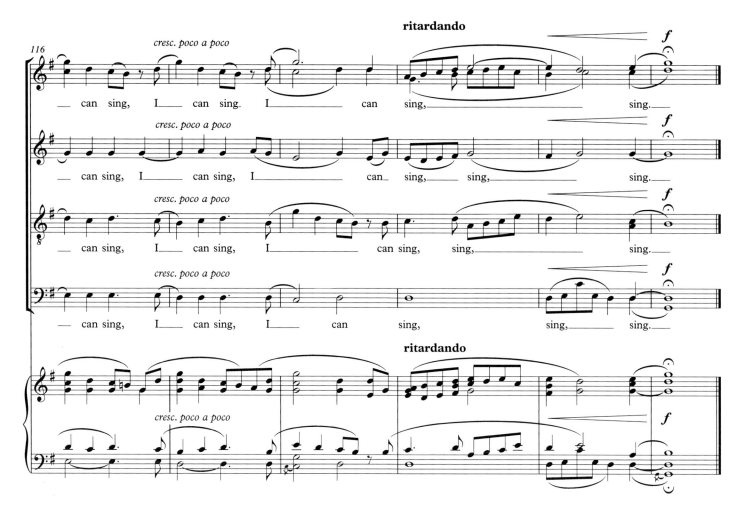